THE NEW BOOK OF

MARS

NIGEL HAWKES

COPPER BEECH BOOKS
BROOKFIELD, CONNECTICUT

Contents

© Aladdin Books Ltd 1998
Designed and produced by
Aladdin Books Ltd
28 Percy Street
London W1P 0LD

First published in the United States in 1998 by
Copper Beech Books,
an imprint of
The Millbrook Press
2 Old New Milford Road
Brookfield, CT 06804

Printed in Belgium
All rights reserved

Editor
Jon Richards
Design
David West
Children's Book Design
Designer
Flick Killerby
Illustrator
Richard Rockwood
Picture Research
Brooks Krikler Research

Library of Congress Cataloging-in-Publication Data
Hawkes, Nigel, 1943
The new book of Mars / Nigel Hawkes ; illustrated by Richard Rockwood.
p. cm.
Includes index.
Summary: Explores the features of the Red Planet, presenting information about the various Pathfinder missions that explored this planetary neighbor.
ISBN 0-7613-0731-1 (pb). — ISBN 0-7613-0811-3 (lib. bdg.)
1. Mars (Planet)—Exploration—Juvenile literature.
2. Mars Pathfinder Project (U.S.)—Juvenile literature.
[1. Mars (Planet) 2. Mars Pathfinder Project (U.S.)]
I. Rockwood, Richard, ill. II. Title.
QB641.H39 1998   97-43126
523.43—dc21   CIP AC
5 4 3 2 1

INTRODUCTION

Often visible in the night sky as a small glowing red star, the planet Mars has long held the human imagination. Long before we had sent the first artificial probes into space, people had created stories about the Red Planet. These have included tales of a planet populated by a warlike race of beings whose mission it was to conquer the earth, or a dying planet whose inhabitants were desperately trying to survive as conditions on their world gradually grew worse.

Since the early 1960s, we have been able to send probes to Mars. They have shown that Mars does not support the civilizations that some people believed. Instead, its barren surface is covered in dust, rocks, huge mountains, and enormous canyons.

Although people now accept that intelligent life has never existed on Mars, recent discoveries have hinted at the presence of much simpler forms of life. The *Viking* missions of the 1970s failed to answer the question fully, while tubelike structures discovered in a meteorite from Mars in 1996 may be the fossilized remains of bacteria. Many scientists now believe that Mars might have supported some form of life and may even do so today.

Beginning with a look at one of the latest missions to the planet, *The New Book of Mars* uses amazing computer illustrations to reproduce our attempts to learn more about the Red Planet. We have found ancient volcanoes, nearly three times higher than any mountain on Earth, and huge chasms, many miles deep, that stretch across nearly half of the planet. Mars has also given us the opportunity to test newer, cheaper ways to travel in space, and it may well prove to be the stepping stone toward our exploration of the solar system.

Return TO MARS

On July 4, 1997, the first spacecraft to visit Mars for more than 20 years made a soft landing in a windswept valley called Ares Vallis. *Mars Pathfinder* had traveled 310 million miles (499 million km) from Earth, carrying the first wheeled vehicle ever sent to any planet. Small, simple, and light, *Pathfinder* cost the U.S. space agency NASA only $265 million, less than a tenth as much as the two *Viking* spacecraft that went to Mars in the 1970s (*see* page 18).

In order to save money, *Pathfinder* needed to be lightweight. As a result, it lacked some of the equipment carried by the *Viking* probes. Unlike its predecessors, *Pathfinder* used only small retro-rockets and parachutes to slow its descent – the *Viking* probes had used much larger parachutes and more powerful rockets to bring them down to the surface safely. To stop *Pathfinder* from being smashed to pieces, scientists developed a landing method involving huge air bags.

The launch of Mars Pathfinder

EARTH TO MARS

Launched on December 4, 1996, *Pathfinder* traveled through space in a compact container (*left*). It then plunged straight into the Martian atmosphere at a speed of 16,000 mph (25,600 km/h), without going into orbit around the planet.

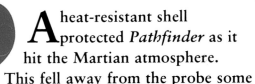

A heat-resistant shell protected *Pathfinder* as it hit the Martian atmosphere. This fell away from the probe some 5 miles (8 km) above the ground, just as parachutes opened to slow the probe's descent to the surface (*left*).

GETTING TO MARS

Pathfinder was fitted on top of a Delta 2 rocket (*left*) and launched from the Kennedy Space Center in Florida (*far bottom left*). Unlike earlier probes, it never went into Earth orbit, but was sent directly to Mars – a flight plan made possible by its light weight. The time of the launch was chosen so that Earth and Mars were as close as possible, reducing the distance that had to be traveled.

During the flight, which took seven months, *Pathfinder* made four correction maneuvers to ensure it was on exactly the right path. As it was cruising through space, the probe continually checked its instruments to ensure that they were operating at peak efficiency when *Pathfinder* reached Mars.

STOPPING THE FALL

As a tether unwound to lower the spacecraft, huge air bags inflated around the probe. Just before impact, three small rockets fired to slow its descent (*left*). With the speed reduced to zero, the tether was cut and *Pathfinder* fell the last 60 ft (20 m) to the ground.

Scientists tested the air bags before the launch of *Pathfinder*. Considering the probe was only the size of a garbage can, this picture (*below*) shows how big the air bags needed to be to protect their contents.

Pathfinder bounced at least a dozen times before it came to rest (*above*). Scientists then had to wait to see if the probe had survived the fall...

Pathfinder ON MARS

After bouncing and rolling to a stop, *Pathfinder* sent out a simple message to indicate that it had come to rest on its base. It landed in a broad Martian valley just 31 miles (50 km) from the site selected three years earlier as the ideal place to start exploring (*below*). Cheers broke out at NASA's Jet Propulsion Laboratory in Pasadena, California, as flight controllers realized that everything had worked perfectly. *Pathfinder* deflated its air bags and opened its three sides, like the petals of a flower. Had it been necessary, these "petals" would have pushed the spacecraft upright.

However, joy soon turned to concern as the controllers realized there were problems. The probe was having difficulties communicating with Earth, while the rover could not get down to the surface of the Red Planet.

Pathfinder landing site

Ares Vallis on Mars

LANDING SITE

Pathfinder landed in the dark, at 3.00 A.M. Mars time. The temperature was a chilly –213°F (–136°C). Six hours later, when the sun had risen above the horizon, *Pathfinder* beamed back the first images, showing a barren and boulder-strewn Martian surface. The lander was then renamed the *Carl Sagan Memorial Station* in honor of the American astronomer who had recently died.

Pathfinder carried a tiny, wheeled vehicle called *Sojourner*, designed to drive down one of the petals onto the Martian surface. No bigger than a microwave oven and weighing 22 lbs (10 kg), *Sojourner* could be commanded from Earth to move around the surface and study particular rocks. It could climb over objects twice the height of its wheels – like driving a car over a kitchen table – or back off automatically and go around if faced with anything bigger than itself.

TEETHING PROBLEMS

The first pictures sent back to Earth showed a
problem; one of the air bags had partially blocked
the end of the petal down
which the rover was to drive
(*above*). That was fixed by
raising and lowering the petal.
In the meantime, problems with communications
were easily solved by resetting a modem.

AIR BAG ROLL MARKS

Some of the first pictures that *Pathfinder* sent
back from the Martian surface were of the marks
that it had made in the rust-colored dirt. These
scratches between the rocks (arrowed, *below*) show
where the air bags surrounding the probe had
scraped along the ground after the spacecraft had
bounced to a landing (*see* pages 4-5). Scientists
were worried that the speed at which the probe
came down to Mars might damage some of the
fragile technology. Luckily,
their fears were unfounded.

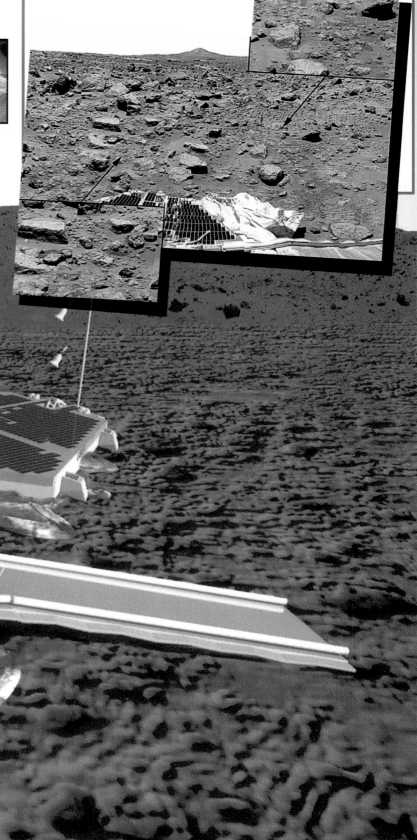

Roving Around

Once the initial problems had been solved (*see* pages 6-7), *Sojourner* was rolled down the ramp and sent to individual rocks to study their makeup. It was able to send back many pictures and a lot of information about the structure and history of the Red Planet.

Mars is much more like Earth than we ever believed. *Pathfinder* found evidence that it once had a warm, wet, and possibly life-supporting climate. Some of the smaller pebbles around the landing site appear to have been rounded by tumbling in water, just like pebbles in a river on Earth. Other stones stick out of larger rocks, suggesting they were cemented together at the bottom of a stream. If so, Mars must have had flowing water, a vital ingredient for the existence of life. Rock analysis also showed other similarities to rocks on Earth that were closer than expected.

THE NEIGHBORHOOD

The area where *Pathfinder* landed shows the effects of floods sweeping across the planet's surface, carrying boulders and smaller stones with them. Rocks of all shapes, sizes, and textures litter the ground (*left*), some similar in composition to rocks on Earth that have been melted by volcanic heat.

Sojourner filmed and analyzed rocks within a few feet of *Pathfinder* (*right*). It sent back more than 500 pictures before contact was lost, by which time *Sojourner* had lasted 12 times longer than its planned lifetime.

TINY ROVER

To keep the mission as inexpensive as possible, the rover had to be made as small as possible (*left*). While it was traveling through space, the rover had to fit into a tiny area that was only 7 in (18 cm) high. Once the probe was on the planet, *Sojourner* could stretch to its full height of 11 in (28 cm). The rover, whose name was chosen by schoolchildren and commemorates a 19th-century African-American reformer, Sojourner Truth, was also 25 in (63 cm) long and 19 in (48 cm) wide.

Building Sojourner

RUNNING ON EMPTY

Pathfinder was designed to last for a month, *Sojourner* for just a week. But they went on sending information for nearly three months before

falling silent. The freezing nights and failing batteries were probably responsible. Once their batteries had run out, they used their solar panels to produce any power they needed. Although this meant that they could not operate during the Martian night, they could still take pictures and send back information to Earth once the sun had risen above the Martian horizon.

Guided by directions sent from Earth, *Sojourner* made its slow progress down the ramps and across the Martian surface (*left*). It could travel over the surface at a mere 0.3 mph (0.5 km/h). Because instructions from Earth took 15 minutes to reach the rover on Mars, scientists had to carefully plan each journey in advance.

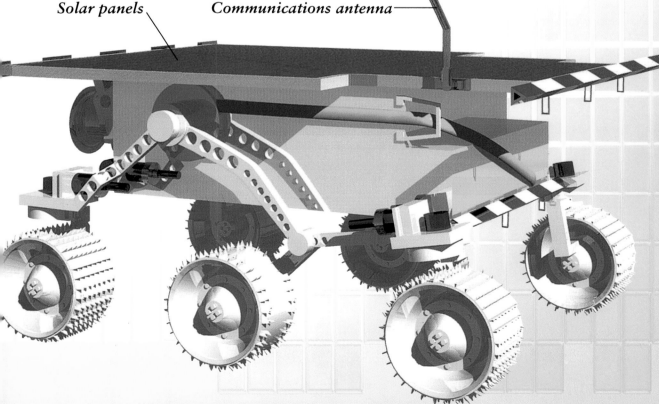

Solar panels   Communications antenna

The rover (*left*) was fitted with many instruments to look at the Martian rocks. The solar panels were used to measure the amount of dust on Martian by comparing the output of clean cells with dusty ones. An Alpha Proton instrument was used to identify chemical elements present in the rocks.

Mars and the SOLAR SYSTEM

Mars is just one of the nine major planets that form the solar system. It is the fourth planet from the sun, lying beyond the orbit of our planet, Earth.

Compared to Earth, Mars is much smaller, a little over half the size. The planet's interior is very similar to Earth's, with a core and mantle surrounded by a thin crust (*below*). The Martian day lasts just over 24 hours, but the year is nearly twice as long as ours.

The planet's surface is also a harsh place. The atmosphere is mostly made up of carbon dioxide and is very thin, barely a hundredth as thick as ours. Dust storms can blanket large parts of the planet for months on end, and it is bitterly cold most of the time, with an average temperature of –9°F (–23°C).

Orbiting the planet are two tiny moons. Scientists believe that they were once free-floating asteroids that originally came from the asteroid belt.

Mantle   Core   Crust

The interior of Mars

Mars has two tiny moons, named Phobos (fear – *see far right*) and Deimos (panic – *right*), after the sons of the Greek god of war. Their small size and the pockmarked shape of the moons suggests that they are probably asteroids trapped by the gravitational pull of Mars.

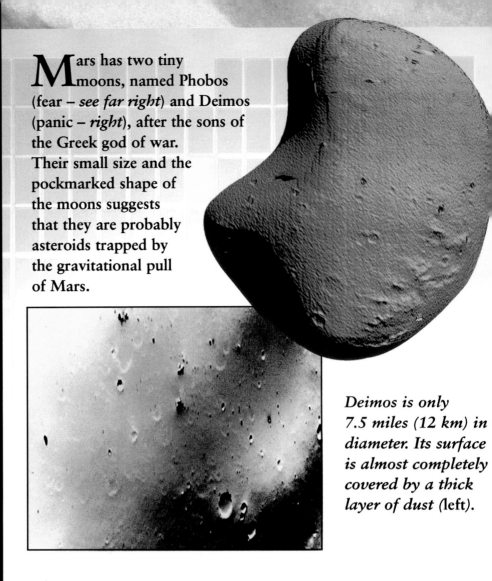

Deimos is only 7.5 miles (12 km) in diameter. Its surface is almost completely covered by a thick layer of dust (left).

CREATING THE SOLAR SYSTEM

The solar system was formed about five billion years ago from a swirling, disk-shaped cloud of dust and gas. When the sun ignited and started to burn as a star, it blew away the lighter gas and dust leaving a disk of heavier dust and rocks. Over time, this swirling disk of material started to join together in clumps (*below*). Larger rocks joined with others until the planets started to take shape. Many of the planets were large enough to hold on to an envelope of gases that formed their atmospheres.

THE SOLAR SYSTEM

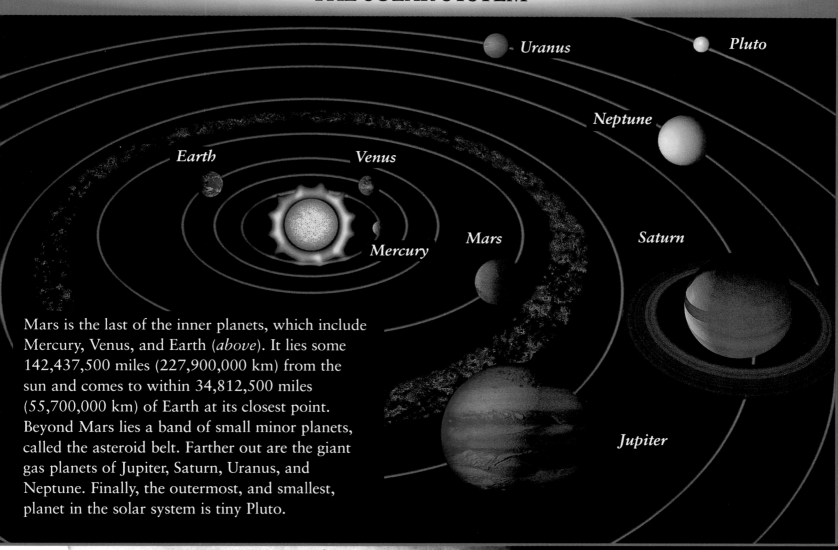

Uranus

Pluto

Neptune

Earth

Venus

Saturn

Mercury

Mars

Jupiter

Mars is the last of the inner planets, which include Mercury, Venus, and Earth (*above*). It lies some 142,437,500 miles (227,900,000 km) from the sun and comes to within 34,812,500 miles (55,700,000 km) of Earth at its closest point. Beyond Mars lies a band of small minor planets, called the asteroid belt. Farther out are the giant gas planets of Jupiter, Saturn, Uranus, and Neptune. Finally, the outermost, and smallest, planet in the solar system is tiny Pluto.

ON THE SURFACE

The surface of Mars is covered with some of the most impressive features in the solar system. Olympus Mons (*left*) is the biggest volcano. It soars 16.5 miles (26.4 km) above the surface – nearly three times the height of Mount Everest.

Phobos (*right*) is the larger of Mars' moons, but it is still only about 14 miles (22 km) in diameter. It orbits Mars every 7.5 hours at a distance of only 3,750 miles (6,000 km), and is slowly spiralling down. In 40 million years it will crash into Mars.

The Red PLANET

Though much smaller than Earth, Mars has no oceans, so its land area is about the same. It is covered with a huge variety of landscapes. These range from the ice caps that cover both poles to huge volcanoes, and from craters ringed by huge cliffs to enormous plains as vast and flat as the Midwest.

For reasons so far unexplained, most of Mars' volcanoes lie in the north, while most of the craters lie in the south. A huge canyon thousands of miles long runs along the Martian equator, stretching over nearly half the planet's circumference.

Many of the names still used for Martian features were devised by the Italian astronomer Schiaparelli, who made a detailed examination of Mars through telescopes (*see* page 14).

MAGNETIC PERSONALITY

A compass on Mars would be little use to help find the way, because there is no global magnetic field. Instead, Mars has patches of magnetism locked into rocks, a remnant of a field that once existed.

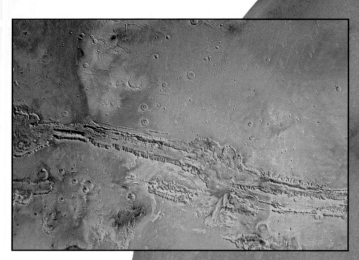

Valles Marineris (*above*) is a huge crack in the surface, 4 miles (6.5 km) deep, and 2,500 miles (4,000 km) in length.

Arabia Terra

Syrtis Major Planitia

FROSTY

The ice covering the poles comes and goes with the seasons. Astronomers have also seen some parts of the planet's surface covered in a light dusting of frost (*left*), just like a winter field on Earth.

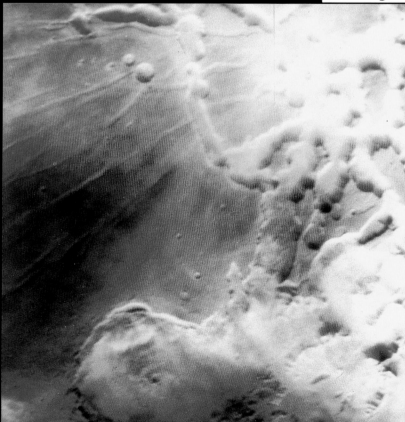

Frost on the surface of Mars

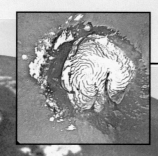

FROZEN POLES

North Polar region

Vastitas Borealis

Viking 2 landing site

Utopia Planitia

Elysium Planitia

Isidis Planitia

Terra Tyrrhena

Mars' northern ice cap (*left* and *below*) is mostly made up from frozen water, while the southern one is made from solid carbon dioxide. The ice at the poles is very thin, only 12 inches (30 cm) at its deepest. With the changing seasons, the caps change in size, and the northern ice cap can be as small as 600 km (375 miles) across.

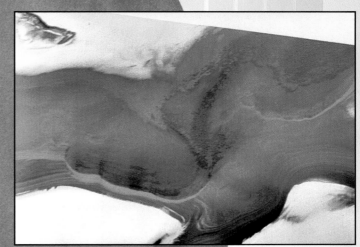

The base of Olympus Mons (*below*) covers the same area as England. Its peak is often surrounded by clouds and the volcanic craters there measure nearly 56 miles (90 km) across.

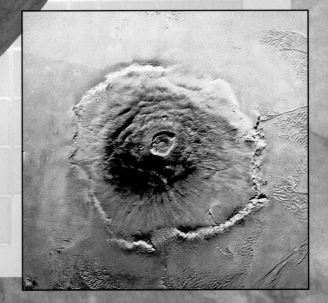

Aliens on MARS

From Earth, Mars appears as a red smudge. Even with telescopes, very little detail can be seen (*below*). Nevertheless, it has gripped our attention, and the lack of detailed knowledge has only encouraged the rumors of alien races there.

In 1877, the Italian astronomer Giovanni Schiaparelli thought he could see channels running across its surface. Later, the American astronomer Percival Lowell made the same claims and said that these "canals" were the work of intelligent Martians, trying to keep a drought-stricken planet alive by drawing water from the poles.

Pictures from the earliest probes to reach Mars demolished the idea of canals and intelligent Martians, but they did pose some curious riddles. Images taken by *Viking 1* from the Cydonia region of Mars seem to show a structure in the rocks resembling a human face. Could this be a trick of the light, or is it a message from a dying civilization?

Mars seen through a telescope on Earth

ALIEN MESSAGE...

The "Face of Mars" (*below*) has started a new controversy. Many people claim that it, and other strangely shaped objects shown on *Viking* images, are signals from a Martian civilization, and that NASA is concealing the facts to prevent panic. These people say that there are eyebrows on the face's forehead and even teeth in the mouth! Using advanced technological 3-D mapping effects, they also point to the presence of a second eye socket which, they say, puts the "trick-of-the-light" theory to rest. The face is surrounded by many other structures which some people believe have also been artificially built. These include a pyramid that is 1600 ft (500 m) high.

SCIENCE FICTION?

Aliens in science fiction are often Martians (*below*), a legacy of the long-held belief that Mars might contain intelligent life. Though no Martians have ever been seen, argument still rages over whether primitive forms of life evolved on Mars, and whether they might exist there today.

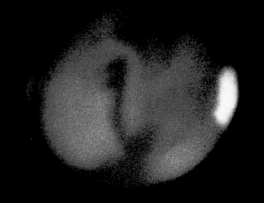

... OR JUST A MOUNTAIN!

Officials and astronomers say that to call the face on Mars a message is nonsense. One explanation is that the human eye is so skilled at recognizing faces that it sees them even in a few shadows. Scientists also point out that every piece of speculation about the "face" is based on two photos sent back from *Viking*. These pictures were so distorted from transmission errors that they had to be digitally adjusted before they were viewed. What we are seeing could just be a trick of the light.

WAR OF THE WORLDS

Written in 1898, H.G. Wells' *War of the Worlds* is a classic of science fiction. It tells the story of an invading force of Martians who try to conquer the world in huge armored tripods. The book has been made into a movie many times, including the 1953 production, where the setting was updated to California in the 1950s (*below*).

On Halloween 1938, a radio broadcast by Orson Welles of *War of the Worlds* (right) was considered so realistic by many people that it caused widespread panic. People actually believed that Earth was being invaded by Martians and ran into the streets in their nightclothes.

Life from MARS?

When it was discovered in 1984 in Antarctica, a meteorite labeled ALH84001 (*below*) was not considered particularly important, even though it was realized that it had originally come from Mars. It lay in storage for several years, before it was examined by a team of scientists. What they found became front-page news around the world. In 1996, the scientists, led by Dr. David McKay, announced that they had found several tubelike structures inside the rock that they believed might be the fossilized remains of ancient bacteria. The rock was formed on Mars some 4.5 billion years ago and was blasted clear of the surface by a huge explosion, possibly a collision with an asteroid, about 15 million years ago (*far right*). It then floated through space before being captured by Earth's gravity and crashing to the ground some 13,000 years ago. Many scientists doubt the claim that these shapes were once bacteria. Instead, they say they could have been formed by geological processes.

Meteorite ALH84001

EARTHLY BACTERIA

Bacteria found on Earth come in many different shapes. This photo (*below*) shows images of fossilized bacteria (colored orange) in rock that may be 3.5 billion years old (colored green). Discovered in rocks from South Africa, these bacteria bear a striking resemblance to the tubelike shapes found in the Martian meteorite (*see below*).

As bacteria go about their business of living, they produce chemicals that might remain within the rock. Careful analysis of these chemicals can show if they are the products of life, or simply chemical processes. But opinions on this still differ.

TELLTALE SIGNS

Dr. McKay's team found tiny globules of chemicals that may have been part of, or produced by, living things. However, recent studies of these chemicals have shown that they entered the rock after it had landed on Earth, and did not come from Mars.

This false-color image of the tubelike structures in the meteorite (colored pink, *right*) shows that they are similar in shape to bacteria on Earth (*see above*) but much smaller. Some results from experiments carried out by the *Viking* probes in the 1970s (*below*) also hinted at the possibility of life. These probes found gases in the soil that may have been given off by bacteria.

Millions of years ago, Mars was bombarded by comets and meteors (below). Their explosions could easily have thrown material up so high that it escaped Mars' gravitational pull and disappeared into space where it was eventually captured by Earth's gravity.

Exploring the PLANET

Because of the fascination that Mars has held, it became a target for investigation by robot probes almost from the very beginning of the space age. The first close-up pictures were sent back in 1965 by *Mariner 4* as it flew past Mars. They provided much more detail than any pictures taken from Earth, which are fuzzy in comparison. They were followed by the orbiting *Mariner 9* probe, which took thousands of images between 1971 and 1972. Together, these two probes destroyed the idea of Martian canals, but showed that Mars was a fascinating place.

The first landings, by *Viking 1* and *Viking 2*, came in 1976, and made measurements of the geology and atmosphere of Mars, while orbiters above took pictures. They showed a rock-strewn landscape tinged with red by iron oxide – rust.

VIKINGS TO MARS

After their launch in Titan-Centaur rockets in 1976, the two *Viking* probes took 11 months to travel to Mars. While the orbiter traveled around the Red Planet, the landers were released to land on the surface (*left*).

The two landers and orbiters sent back hundreds of images and lots of information about Mars. They continued to work for many years beyond their planned lifetime.

Viking 1 landed on a rocky plain, Chryse Planitia, 22° north of the Martian equator, and *Viking 2* on Utopia Planitia, 48° north and on the other side of the planet (*see* page 13). They measured atmospheric pressure (very low) and found that the atmosphere was 95 percent carbon dioxide, with only traces of water vapor. Both landers scooped up soil and found it was an iron-rich clay, containing no organic compounds. Biological experiments showed changes hinting at life, but these could be explained as a simple chemical reaction.

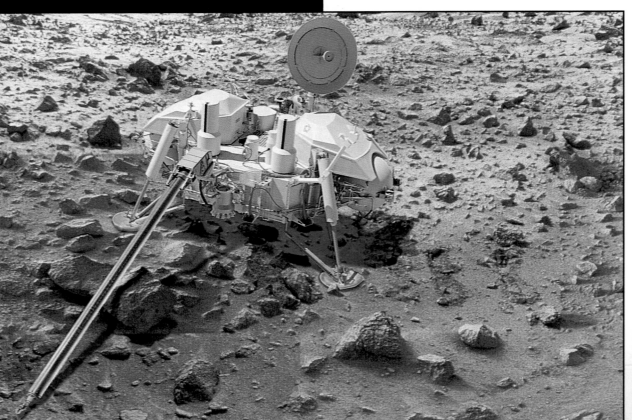

The Viking *lander*

The Viking *landers were nearly 7 ft (2 m) high and weighed over half a ton (left). An extendible arm collected samples of soil for analysis. Pictures from one of the landers came back at a slight angle, indicating that it had landed on uneven ground (below).*

MARINER 9

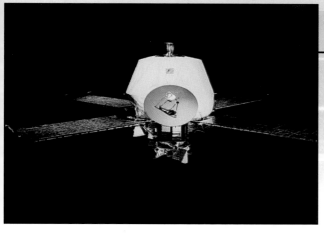

Mariner 9

Mariner 9 (*left*) reached Mars in November 1971. During its mission, it took more than 7,000 pictures, found that Mars has seasons, and identified huge features such as the Valles Marineris, named after the mission.

The *Mariner* images of Mars showed it to be far from dull. This image (*right*), sent back by *Mariner 9*, shows what might be a dried-up water channel.

MARINER 4

Mariner 4 (*below*) was launched on November 28, 1964 and took seven months to reach Mars. It weighed 575 lbs (260 kg) and carried a television camera and six other instruments, including a cosmic ray telescope, to study the planet and the region of space between it and Earth.

Mariner 4 sent back 22 pictures as the probe swept past the planet. Its closest approach was on July 14, 1965, when it passed within 6,118 miles (9,879 km) of Mars. As it disappeared behind the planet, the changes in the probe's signals allowed scientists to calculate the density and temperature of the Martian atmosphere.

Mariner 4

Failed MISSIONS

Mars has been a jinxed planet, especially for the Russians. Between 1960 and 1973, they made more than a dozen attempts to reach Mars, with very little success. The spacecraft either lost contact with Earth, crash-landed, or missed Mars altogether. More recently, two probes to the moon Phobos also failed. *Phobos 1* was lost on the way to Mars in 1988, while *Phobos 2* reached Mars and sent back some useful data before its signal was lost in March 1989. Then, in 1996, Russia's most recent attempt failed when the rocket carrying their *Mars '96* probe exploded without even reaching Earth orbit.

The United States has done a little better, with orbiting probes and landers on the planet's surface (*see* pages 18-19). But in 1993, *Mars Observer* (*below*) blew up when it was within sight of the planet.

Mars Observer *leaves Earth orbit*

MARS OBSERVER

After launch, the *Mars Observer* probe cruised for almost one year toward Mars (*above* and *below*). It was due to enter an oval orbit around the planet and then fire retro-rockets to enter a circular orbit. However, the probe went silent just short of Mars.

MARS '96

Mars '96, which exploded spectacularly in the Earth's atmosphere, consisted of an orbiter that was to study the surface of Mars and its atmosphere (*left*). This orbiter carried a number of ball-shaped modules that were to be dropped to the surface. Once on Mars, four petals were to open and align the module correctly, regardless of how it landed (*below left*). The module was then to send back information and high-quality television pictures of Mars via the orbiting probe.

Russia has launched 19 missions to Mars, of which only two, *Zond 3* in 1965 and *Mars 5* in 1973, were successful. Both returned pictures, though of a lower quality than those sent back by the *Mariner* probes.

Mars 2 and *Mars 3*, launched by the Soviet Union in May 1971, were designed to make soft landings on Mars. Both landed, but *Mars 2* sent no signals, presumably because of impact damage.

Mars 3 landed in the middle of a dust storm that dragged it across the surface (*below*). It sent data for only 20 seconds. The United States has sent 11 missions, of which only three have been complete failures (*see right*).

MISSING IN ACTION

Some 20 missions to the Red Planet have ended in disaster. The total list of failed probes to Mars is –

U.S. missions:
Mariner 3; *Mariner 8*; and *Mars Observer*.

Russian missions:
Five unnamed missions; *Mars 1*; *Zond 2*; *Zond 8*; *Kosmos 419*; *Mars 2*; *Mars 3*; *Mars 4*; *Mars 6*; *Mars 7*; *Phobos 1*; *Phobos 2*; and *Mars '96*.

Mars Global SURVEYOR

After the failure of the *Mars Observer* in 1993 (*see* page 20), a new, much cheaper mission was quickly planned. *Mars Global Surveyor* was designed to use spare hardware from *Observer*. It was built to be lighter than *Observer*, so that it could be launched by a Delta 2 rocket (*below*) and do almost the same job at a quarter of the cost.

One big saving was in the fuel carried by *Surveyor*. *Mars Observer* had been fitted with massive fuel tanks and powerful retro-rockets that were to put the probe in a circular orbit around Mars. Instead of using these, *Surveyor* was designed to exploit the friction of the thin Martian upper atmosphere. As *Surveyor* orbited the planet it dipped into Mars' atmosphere where it was slowed by "aerobraking." This slowing down brought the probe into the correct orbit.

ALL-SEEING EYE

Mars Global Surveyor was put together and tested at NASA's Kennedy Space Center (*above*). It has the capacity to take incredibly sharp images – so good it may even see the *Viking* and *Pathfinder* landers sitting on the surface. *Surveyor* has already made observations of Mars' magnetic field, finding areas of strong magnetism as if the surface were littered with small but powerful magnets pointing different ways.

AROUND THE BLOCK

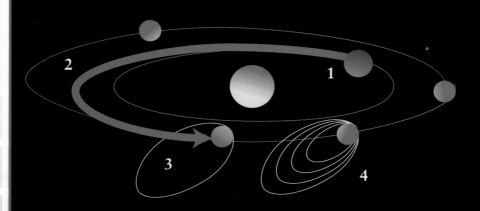

Mars Global Surveyor was launched from Earth on November 7, 1996 (1 – *above*). After traveling through space for ten months (2) it entered an elliptical, or oval, orbit around Mars (3). Over the next four months, *Surveyor* undertook aerobraking maneuvers (*see right*) designed to bring the space probe down into a circular orbit around the planet (4).

A circular orbit is very important for *Mars Global Surveyor*. Only by keeping its distance from Mars constant can it map and measure the Martian surface accurately. The probe will study Mars for about two Earth years.

Global Surveyor reached Mars on schedule on September 11, 1997, but problems soon arose. A latch on one of its long solar panels (*below*) was damaged during launch. This caused the spacecraft to wobble as it dipped to within 70 miles (110 km) of the surface. To reduce stress, aerobraking will be slowed, and the mapping of Mars will now start in March 1999, a year later than planned.

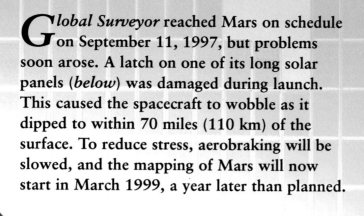

Unlike normal cameras on Earth, the camera on *Surveyor* has no moving parts. In order to focus it, small heaters behind one of the mirrors in the camera are turned on and off. The warmth from these heaters causes the mirror to bend and warp very slightly, adjusting the focus of the image. The camera is so accurate that it will be able to see objects that are less than 3 ft (1 m) in diameter.

Surveyor's solar panels are also its brakes. Each time Mars Global Surveyor passes close to the planet, friction and drag from Mars' upper atmosphere cause the probe to slow down (above). This friction also causes the solar panels to heat up. Fortunately, the solar panels are designed to resist temperatures up to 374°F (190°C).

Surveyor '98

Every 26 months, Earth and Mars move into the best alignment to launch spacecraft. In late 1998 and early 1999, two craft will be launched by NASA – an orbiter and a lander. Together, they form a single mission, called *Mars Surveyor '98*. The orbiter will act as a relay station for the lander's data, and, at the same time, it will map areas of the planet's surface. The two probes will also study the Martian climate, and explore the southern polar region where the lander will come down. Here they will measure the amount of water and carbon dioxide in the ice cap. Even smaller than *Mars Pathfinder*, the two spacecraft will cost $92 million and can be launched on a new, low-cost rocket.

Once the mission has been completed, the orbiter will remain functional as it goes around the planet. It may then be used as a signal relay for future Mars missions over the next two or three years.

The *Mars Surveyor '98* orbiter (*main picture*), due for launch in December 1998, will go into orbit around the poles of Mars.

During its lifetime, it will monitor daily weather conditions on the planet, measure the temperature of the atmosphere at different heights, and take high-resolution images of the surface. It will also relay data from the lander.

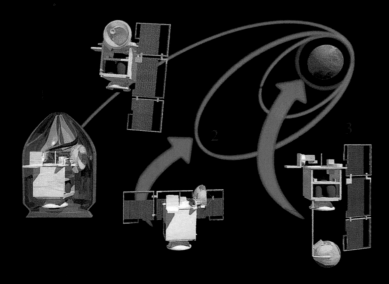

The orbiter will be launched on top of a Delta rocket (1 – *left*). Using the same method of "aerobraking" used in the *Mars Global Surveyor* mission (*see* page 23), the orbiter will enter Mars' orbit in an elliptical, or oval path (2). This will gradually become circular as the probe slows down with each skim of the atmosphere. Once it is in orbit over Mars' poles (3), the mission can begin and the lander will arrive on the surface.

The lander, due for launch in January 1999 (1 – *above*), will reach Mars in December 1999. It will land softly with the aid of thrusters and a parachute. As it descends (2), it will release probes that will plunge like daggers into the surface of the planet, providing data about what lies below.

Once it has landed on the surface, the lander will spread its solar panels and begin work (3). It has robot arms to collect samples and it will carry two small microprobes that will penetrate the Martian soil to find frozen water.

MARS SURVEYOR '98

PROJECT TIMETABLE

1998
December 10 – Launch of *Mars Surveyor '98* orbiter
1999
January 3 – Launch of *Mars Surveyor '98* lander
September 23 – Orbiter enters elliptical orbit around Mars
December 1 – Orbiter enters circular mapping orbit
December 3 – Lander reaches surface of Mars
2000
February 29 – Mission on planet's surface ends
March 3 – Orbiter begins mapping Mars
2002
January 15 – Orbiter acts as relay for future Mars missions
2004
December 1 – Mission ends

Future MISSIONS

The next ten years will see a period of intense exploration of Mars, with up to a dozen missions visiting the planet. Never before has such a concentrated effort been made to understand and explore another planet. All of this information will pave the way for humans to visit Mars.

NASA, having shown that small spacecraft can be inexpensive and effective, plans missions in the next three launch windows of 2001, 2003, and 2005. It will also cooperate with Russia on a joint mission in 2001. Japan plans a launch in 1998, while the European Space Agency is hoping to use spare instruments from the unsuccessful Russian *Mars '96* probe for its own *Mars Express* mission. One of these missions may even send back samples of Martian rock, direct from the surface of the planet.

MISR – short for Mars In-situ-Utilization Sample Return – is designed to collect and return samples of Martian rock. A rover vehicle carried on the lander will collect the samples and return them to the lander. In the meantime, the lander will create its own oxygen and fuel from the Martian atmosphere, creating the fuel for its return journey. It will take about 580 days to fill its fuel tanks and then blast off back to Earth with the rock samples (*right*).

Only by retrieving Martian samples will it be possible to prove or disprove whether life exists on the Red Planet. The earliest date for that is 2005, when NASA plans to bring rocks, soil, and atmospheric gases back to Earth.

The French balloon (*right*) may carry a long, snakelike probe that will study the Martian rocks and soil. As the balloon cruises close to the surface during the Martian night, this probe will drag along the ground collecting data.

PLANET B

Due to be launched in 1998, the Japanese probe *Planet B* will measure an area of Mars that has never been closely looked at before – the upper atmosphere. Using 11 instruments, the probe will study the region where the upper limits of Mars' atmosphere interact with the charged particles that continuously stream out of the sun, called the solar wind. *Planet B* will also carry a radar instrument to look for unseen deposits of water that may lie beneath the Martian surface.

COME FLY WITH ME

The French have designed a balloon that will travel over the Martian terrain (*left*). During the day, heat from the sun will cause the balloon's gases to expand, making it climb high into the atmosphere. At night, when the temperatures are cooler, the balloon will sink back down toward the ground.

In 1998, a planned Russian mission was postponed for lack of money. Now it could fly, possibly in 2001, as the first joint Russian and American planetary probe, called *Mars Together*. This would involve a large Russian rover (*right*), launched by a rocket. But it would be carried inside a spacecraft made in the United States. They would simultaneously launch an orbiter to provide communications.

People on MARS

Putting people on Mars is possible, but it will be very expensive. Using the methods developed for the *Apollo* Moon landings in the late 1960s and early 1970s, a mission to Mars might cost as much as $400 billion.

However, there is a cheaper alternative – using Mars itself to provide the fuel for the trip home, saving the cost of taking fuel there. First, a 40-ton robot factory would be sent to Mars. Powered by a nuclear reactor, it would take carbon dioxide from the air and water frozen in the ice at the poles. It would turn these into methane and oxygen to power the rocket on its return trip to Earth. Once sufficient fuel had been collected, a crew of astronauts would then be sent to Mars, safe in the knowledge that their return trip had already been booked. This approach, called *Mars Direct*, could cut the cost to only $50 billion.

ROBOT FACTORY

Sent in advance, the robot factory craft (*above*) would carry hydrogen, needed to make methane from carbon dioxide found in the Martian atmosphere. The by-product would be water, which would be electrolyzed to make oxygen and more hydrogen. In less than a year, such a plant could create 108 tons of methane and oxygen for the return journey to Earth.

With the fuel ready for the return mission, humans would be sent to Mars (*right*) and land near the robot factory craft. For the next eighteen months, these people would explore and study the planet (*below*). At the next launch window, the astronauts would then return to Earth with any samples that they had collected.

It is believed that such a mission could be launched within ten years, at a cost of only a fifth of NASA's annual budget.

During their long stay on the Red Planet, the astronauts would explore the Martian surface and study the rocks and soil (above). They may also look for minerals that would make the mining of Mars a commercial prospect.

TERRAFORMING

The first permanent bases on Mars would be sealed space stations. But one day it may be possible to turn Mars into an imitation Earth by using the gases that cause global warming here on Earth such as carbon dioxide. This process is called "terraforming." By adding more of these gases to the Martian atmosphere, they would trap heat, warm up the planet, melt the water, and liberate carbon dioxide in the ice caps. This would alter the atmosphere so that it was like Earth's millions of years ago.

Primitive bacteria could then be introduced and grown on the planet. Over the space of many years, perhaps even thousands, these would create enough oxygen to produce an atmosphere that we could breathe and a planet covered with plants and oceans (*below*).

Glossary & TIMELINE

Aerobraking
A method of slowing a spacecraft by getting it to skim through a planet's upper atmosphere. The spacecraft is slowed by friction and drag created as it passes through the gases.

Asteroid
A small, rocky object that orbits the sun, also called a minor planet. Most asteroids are found in the asteroid belt, a region of space between Mars and Jupiter.

Astronauts
People who travel into space. Russian astronauts are called cosmonauts.

Astronomers
People who study the stars and planets.

Atmosphere
A layer of gases that surrounds a planet. Mars' atmosphere is very thin compared to Earth's and mostly consists of carbon dioxide.

Core
The very center of a planet.

Crust
The outermost section of a planet's structure. It sits on top of the mantle.

Equator
The part of a planet that runs around its middle. It lies halfway between the two poles.

Gravity
The attractive force of a body. The larger or more dense the body, the greater its gravitational force. A large body, such as the sun, will have a higher gravitational force than Earth.

Lander
The part of a spacecraft that lands on a planet's surface.

Launch window
A period when two planets are in ideal positions to launch a spacecraft from one to the other.

Mantle
The part of a planet's interior that surrounds the core.

Meteorite
A rocky object that comes from space and crashes onto Earth's surface.

Moons
Small bodies that orbit around some of the major planets.

NASA
Short for National Aeronautics and Space Administration, it is the organization that runs all of the United States' missions into space.

1976
Viking *probes land on Mars*

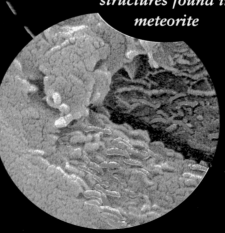

1996
Tubelike structures found in meteorite

Orbit

The path of a body around another, central body such as the orbit of a planet around a star. Mars takes 687 days to go around the sun.

Orbiter

The part of a spacecraft that orbits a planet.

Planets

Bodies that travel around a star.

Probes

Robot devices that explore and study space.

Rover

The part of a spacecraft that explores a planet's surface. Most rovers today are controlled by instructions sent from Earth.

Satellites

Objects that orbit a planet. These can be natural, such as moons, or artificial, such as communications satellites.

Solar panels

The parts of spacecraft that convert sunlight into electricity that the spacecraft can use to power its different functions.

Solar system

The group of major planets, including Earth, and minor planets that orbit the sun.

Telescope

An object that, when looked through, enlarges images. Astronomers use telescopes to study planets and stars.

Terraforming

The process of turning an uninhabitable planet into one that resembles Earth, where humans can live without the need for sealed space stations.

Volcano

A hole in a planet's crust through which liquid rock pours onto the surface in an eruption. Mars has many volcanoes, but they are all extinct and have not erupted for many thousands of years.

1971
Mariner 9 *starts to orbit Mars*

1965
Mariner 4 *sends back first close-ups of Mars*

1997
Mars Pathfinder *probe lands on Mars*

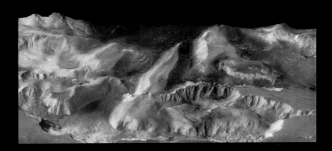

Index

PHOTO CREDITS:

Abbreviations: t-top, m-middle, b-bottom, r-right, l-left
All the pictures in this book are by NASA except on the following pages:
2, 4b, 20 all, 25, 29m, 30-31 & back cover bottom – Frank Spooner Pictures. 3b & 14 –
Mary Evans Picture Library. 15bm & br – Kobal Collection. 16 both, 18bl, 21 both, 28t, 28-29
& 30 both –Science Photo Library. 17 – Galaxy Picture Library.